INVENT IT

REPURPOSE IT

INVENT NEW USES FOR OLD STUFF

by Tammy Enz

Project Consultant
Daniel Enz, P.E. PhD
Assistant Professor, General Engineering
University of Wisconsin, Platteville

CAPSTONE PRESS
a capstone imprint

Fact Finders Books are published by Capstone Press,
1710 Roe Crest Drive, North Mankato, Minnesota 56003
www.capstonepub.com

Books published by Capstone Press are manufactured with paper
containing at least 10 percent post-consumer waste.

Library of Congress Cataloging-in-Publication Data
Enz, Tammy.
  Repurpose it : invent new uses for old stuff / by Tammy Enz.
    p. cm.—(Fact finders. Invent it)
  Includes bibliographical references and index.
  Summary: "Explains the principles of inventing and provides photo-illustrated instructions for making
a variety of projects that recycle and reuse materials"—Provided by publisher.
  ISBN 978-1-4296-7636-6 (library binding)
  ISBN 978-1-4296-7983-1 (paperback)
  1. Refuse and refuse disposal—Juvenile literature. 2. Recycling (Waste, etc.)—Juvenile literature. 3.
Conservation projects (Natural resources)—Juvenile literature. 4. Conservation of natural resources—
Juvenile literature. I. Title. II. Series.
  TD792.E69 2012
  600—dc23   2011028738

Editorial Credits
Christopher L. Harbo, editor; Sarah Bennett, designer; Eric Gohl, media researcher; Marcy Morin,
    scheduler; Sarah Schuette, photo stylist; Laura Manthe, production specialist

Photo Credits
Capstone Studio: Karon Dubke, all cover and interior project photos
Shutterstock: badah, 8 (bottom), bcdan, 21 (bottom), joingate, 24 (bottom), Petr Malyshev, 18

Design Elements
Shutterstock: alekup, liskus, Sylverarts, Tropinina Olga

Printed in the United States of America in Brainerd, Minnesota.
102011   006406BANGS12

CONTENTS

RADICAL RECYCLING

It's fun, it's free, and it's green! Inventing new uses for old stuff is a great challenge for engineers and inventors. Today people are using up a lot of **natural resources** and making lots and lots of garbage. Finding uses for all that garbage can lead to some awesome Earth-saving inventions. Get ready to raid your recycle bin. Your inventions will breathe new life into old stuff.

THE SIX STEPS OF INVENTING

Engineers and inventors follow a certain method when inventing. This method helps them build on their successes and learn from their failures. Inventors call the method's steps by different names, but the basics are always the same. Follow these six steps to see how inventing works:

natural resource—any substance found in nature that people use, such as soil, air, trees, coal, and oil

THE SIX STEPS OF INVENTING

1 PROBLEM
2 PROPERTIES
3 IDEAS
4 PLAN
5 CREATE
6 IMPROVE

1 PROBLEM Inventors usually start with a problem. Ask yourself—What problem am I trying to solve?

2 PROPERTIES Properties are the special characteristics of an object. An object's properties could include its color, shape, and size. Properties could also include what an object is made of and how it can be used. Ask yourself—What useful properties does an object have that could help solve my problem?

3 IDEAS Write down some ideas that could help solve your problem. Be creative. Then pick the idea you think will work the best.

4 PLAN Plan how to build your device. Gather the tools and supplies needed.

5 CREATE Put everything together and make something new.

6 IMPROVE Once the solution is created, ask yourself if it solved the problem. If not, what can you change? If so, how can you make it better?

For each invention you build, the process starts all over again. Let's see these six steps in action with the inventions in this book.

Compost Bin

1 PROBLEM Humans are eating machines. But there's often scraps of food left over after a meal. Can you come up with a use for food scraps?

2 PROPERTIES What useful properties does leftover food have? It is **biodegradable**, full of nutrients, and tasty to bugs and critters.

3 IDEAS Are you thinking food fight? Pet food? Or how about compost for **fertilizing** the garden? Raw fruit and vegetable scraps make great compost for your garden.

4 PLAN Gather together:
- ✔ plastic 5-gallon (19-liter) bucket with a lid
- ✔ drill
- ✔ ¾-inch (1.9-centimeter) drill bit
- ✔ grass clippings
- ✔ raw fruit and vegetable scraps
- ✔ garden spade

biodegradable—a substance or object that breaks down naturally in the environment
fertilize—to make soil rich and healthy

1 Turn the bucket upside down. Have an adult drill 20 holes randomly in the bottom of the bucket.

2 Turn the bucket upright. Place it in a warm outdoor place on bare soil.

3 Place a few inches of grass clippings in the bottom of the bucket.

4 Add a layer of raw fruit and vegetable scraps. Then add more yard waste. Place the lid on the bucket.

5 Periodically add layers of fruit and vegetable scraps and grass clippings. Use a garden spade to stir the top layers each time you add more scraps.

CONTINUED ON NEXT PAGE ➡

6 Keep the material in the bucket damp by sprinkling water on it every few days.

7 In a few weeks, the scraps and grass clippings will break down into rich compost for your garden.

6 IMPROVE

Did your fruit and vegetable scraps turn into compost? The scraps on the bottom of the bucket break down first. Can you design a trap door to remove this compost while leaving the rest?

➡ COMPOST THIS

In the 1890s, New York City had two big problems. First, it had a lot of garbage with nowhere to put it. Second, it needed more land to build an immigration center on Ellis Island. It didn't take long before someone decided to repurpose the garbage. The city began dumping dirt, bricks, and garbage in the water. Soon the size of Ellis Island increased from 3.3 acres (1.3 hectares) to 27.5 acres (11 hectares). A hundred years ago dumping garbage in New York harbor seemed like a good idea. Now people know that garbage is harmful to sea animals.

Cool Can Can Cooler

CONTINUED ON NEXT PAGE ➡

1 PROBLEM Soup, vegetables, and spaghetti sauce all come in heavy-duty tin cans. Don't let all those cans go out with the recycling. Can you invent a way to repurpose them?

2 PROPERTIES What are some of the useful properties of cans? Cans are sturdy and strong, they are waterproof, and they can hold food and liquids. Different sizes can also be stacked together.

3 IDEAS Cans make good storage containers for all types of objects and foods. They are also stackable and can hold liquids. Perhaps two cans and some water can be assembled and frozen to make a cool and useful can cooler.

4 PLAN

Gather together:
- ✔ 15-ounce (425-gram) tin can
- ✔ foam meat tray, washed
- ✔ pencil
- ✔ scissors
- ✔ drill
- ✔ ³⁄₁₆-inch (.5-cm) drill bit
- ✔ 28-ounce (794-g) tin can
- ✔ ½-inch (1.3-cm) long x ³⁄₁₆-inch (.5-cm) diameter bolt and nut
- ✔ screwdriver

1 Place the small can on the tray and draw a circle around it with a pencil. Make the circle slightly larger than the can. Cut out the circle.

2 With an adult's help, drill a hole in the center of both cans' bottoms.

3 Punch a hole into the center of the foam circle with the drill bit.

4 Insert the bolt through the hole in the bottom of the large can.

5 Place the foam piece into the large can. Allow the bolt sticking through the bottom of the can to slide through the hole in the foam.

6 Place the small can on top of the foam inside the large can. Slide the bolt through the bottom of the small can.

7 On the inside of the small can, place the nut on the bolt. Tighten it with your fingers. Then use the screwdriver to tighten the bolt as much as you can.

8 Fill the space between the two cans with water. Leave about 1 inch (2.5 cm) unfilled at the top.

9 Place the can cooler into the freezer until the water is frozen. Remove the can cooler and place a can of soda in it.

6 IMPROVE

How long does the can cooler keep your soda cool? Try making several can coolers. Paint or decorate them each differently. Use them at a party so people can tell their drinks apart. Think of ways to make a larger cooler that can hold more than one can.

Solar Still

1 PROBLEM Most of Earth's surface is covered with saltwater oceans. But none of this water is drinkable. Can you invent a way to take the salt out of salt water so you can drink it?

2 PROPERTIES Salt water has most of the same properties as drinkable water, except for the salt. Because salt water is like drinkable water, it will freeze, boil, and **evaporate**.

3 IDEAS Are any of these properties useful in removing salt? Freezing probably won't work. Boiling and evaporation might separate the salt from the water. But these processes release the water as a gas and leave the salt behind. Can you find a way to capture the gas and change it back into a liquid?

4 PLAN Gather together:
- ✔ large mixing bowl
- ✔ warm water
- ✔ ¼ cup (60 mL) of salt
- ✔ spoon
- ✔ heavy drinking glass (must be shorter than the bowl)
- ✔ washed marbles
- ✔ plastic wrap
- ✔ masking tape
- ✔ small rock
- ✔ desk lamp

evaporate—to change from a liquid into a vapor or a gas
condense—to change from gas to liquid; water vapor condenses into liquid water

1 Fill the bowl about half full of water. Add the salt. Stir the mixture until the salt is dissolved.

2 Set the glass in the center of the bowl. The water level must be below the top of the glass. Place washed marbles inside the glass to weigh it down.

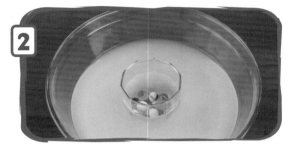

3 Wrap the plastic wrap tightly over the top of the bowl. Tape down the edges of the plastic wrap to make sure it stays tight over the bowl.

4 Place the small rock on top of the plastic wrap. The plastic wrap should slope downward toward the middle of the glass. Then place the bowl under a desk lamp.

5 The heat from the lamp will cause the water to evaporate. The evaporated water will **condense** on the plastic and drip into the glass. When enough water has collected in the glass, remove the plastic wrap and marbles, and take a drink.

6 IMPROVE

Do you taste any salt? Try this invention to see if it also works to remove dirt from muddy water. Could you use the same idea to capture water from the ground in a desert?

Buzzy Bug Bot

1 PROBLEM Most people get a new cell phone every couple of years. That leaves a lot of old phones lying around. Can you come up with any new uses for old cell phones?

2 PROPERTIES Old cell phones have many parts that can be repurposed. They have batteries, speakers, lights, and a vibrating motor.

3 IDEAS You can wire up all kinds of electronic gizmos, such as flashlights and buzzers, with cell phone parts. You can also use the vibrating motor to make a tiny robot.

4 PLAN

Gather together:
- ✔ old cell phone
- ✔ small screwdriver
- ✔ needle-nose pliers
- ✔ sandpaper
- ✔ 2 pieces of 30 gauge enamel coated wire, 2½-inch (6 cm) long
- ✔ tin snips
- ✔ flat-bristled toothbrush
- ✔ small binder clip
- ✔ small rubber band
- ✔ scissors
- ✔ plastic milk jug
- ✔ pencil
- ✔ hot glue gun and glue
- ✔ 2 medium-sized googly eyes
- ✔ 1.5 volt circular watch battery

1 Remove the back and the battery from the cell phone. Unscrew the small screws to open the phone. Look for a small **cylindrical** motor about ½-inch (1.3-cm) long. It will have a moon-shaped end.

2 Remove any parts connected to the motor. Find the two small metal flaps on the motor. Bend these flaps slightly away from the motor with the pliers. Be careful not to bend them too far.

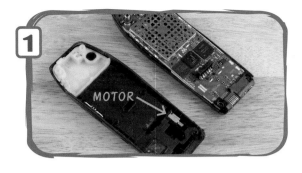

3 Use the sandpaper to remove about ¼ inch (.6 cm) of enamel from the ends of each of the wires.

4 Bend one end of one wire into a very small loop. Place the loop around one of the flaps on the motor. Use the pliers to bend the flap back into place.

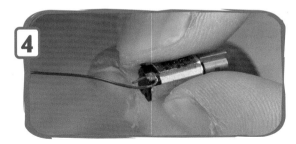

5 Repeat step 4 with the other wire and the other flap.

CONTINUED ON NEXT PAGE ➡

cylindrical—to have flat, circular ends and sides shaped like the outside of a tube

6 With an adult's help, use tin snips to clip off the toothbrush handle. Discard the handle.

7 Set the binder clip on its edge on top of the toothbrush. The clip's handles should hang off the front edge of the toothbrush.

8 Wrap the rubber band around the clip and the brush to hold them together.

9 Cut a flat piece of plastic from the milk jug with a scissors. Fold it in half. Sketch out a wing on the plastic with a pencil. The wing should be about 1½ inches (4 cm) long. Make it about ¼ inch (.6 cm) wide at the fold and 1 inch (2.5 cm) at its tip.

10 Cut out the wings and unfold them.

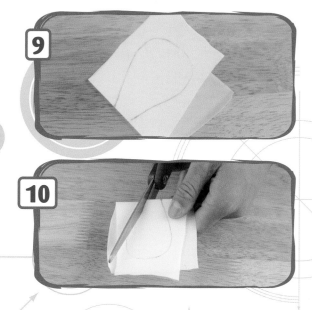

11 Hot glue the wings near the back of the toothbrush head.

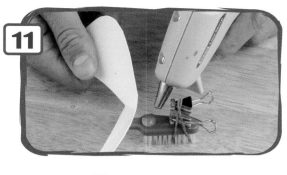

12 Hot glue googly eyes to the handles of the binder clip.

13 Open the binder clip and insert the battery in the clip.

14 Carefully fit the wires into the clip. One wire should be on either side of the battery to complete a circuit.

15 The motor will begin vibrating. Place the bug on a flat surface and let it go.

CONTINUED ON NEXT PAGE ➤

6 *IMPROVE*

Does your bug bot buzz across the table? Check all your connections. Reposition the clip to keep the bug balanced. Try moving the buzzing motor up and down. Move it closer to the bug's body. Does its move faster?

➡ **WHEN IN NEED–INVENT!**

When Chester Greenwood got ice skates for his 15th birthday, he never thought they'd change his life. When he went out to use them, his ears got so cold they turned blue. He tried wearing a scarf on his ears, but it was too itchy. Then he sewed some fur to baling wire loops. When he connected the loops together, he had earmuffs! People loved his idea. He started an earmuff factory. Soon his hometown of Farmington, Maine, was the earmuff capital of the world, and Chester was famous.

Textbook Safe

1 PROBLEM Textbooks are best for reading. But do they have any other uses when they are out-of-date? Can you come up with a way to reuse an old textbook?

2 PROPERTIES Textbooks are made from paper which has many uses. And they are heavy, thick, and fit nicely on a shelf.

3 IDEAS You could shred the pages and use them for stuffing. Or you could use the book for a doorstop. But what if you carve out a book's center and make it into a hidden safe to store your valuables? Would anyone suspect that a textbook sitting on a shelf is holding hidden treasure?

4 PLAN

Gather together:
- ✔ old, thick hardcover book
- ✔ ruler
- ✔ pencil
- ✔ utility knife
- ✔ glue stick

CONTINUED ON NEXT PAGE ➡

1 Open the book so you have about ½ inch (1.3 cm) of pages on the left side.

2 On the right side, use the ruler and pencil to measure and mark lines 1½ inches (3.8 cm) from each of the four sides of the top page. These lines will form a rectangle on the center of the page.

3 Have an adult use the utility knife to cut through several pages along the edges of this rectangle. Remove the pieces that have been cut loose.

4 Continue cutting a few pages at a time, until there are only about 20 pages remaining.

5 Use the glue stick to coat the inside of the opening and the outside of the pages with a thin layer of glue.

6 When the glue is dry, place your valuables inside. Shut the cover and place the book on a shelf. No one will guess what is hidden inside.

Does your textbook safe hide all your treasures? Can you come up with a clasp for the book so only you can open it?

➡ TREASURE IN THE TRASH

The Frisbie Baking Company made pies and sold them in tin pans in the early 1900s. Students at Yale University would eat the pies and then play catch with the tins. This campus fad was called "frisbie-ing." Later a toy company started making plastic flying disks. The company workers didn't know the origin of frisbie-ing, but kept the name Frisbee anyway.

Lawn Chair Seat

1 PROBLEM When you buy eight-packs of drink bottles, you get plastic eight-pack rings. If not thrown away properly, these rings can be harmful to wildlife that gets stuck in them. Can you repurpose eight-pack rings to keep them out of the trash?

2 PROPERTIES What useful properties do these rings have? They are strong, flexible, and good for organizing things.

3 IDEAS You could hang an eight-pack ring from a nail to make a closet organizer for socks and underwear. You could attach a handle to the rings to make a bubble wand. Or you could use these strong, flexible rings to make a new seat for an old lawn chair.

4 PLAN

Gather together:
- ✔ scissors
- ✔ old lawn chair
- ✔ tape measure
- ✔ pencil
- ✔ paper
- ✔ plastic eight-pack rings
- ✔ plastic zip ties

5 CREATE

1 Use the scissors to cut away the old fabric seat from the chair.

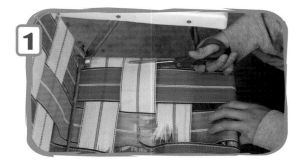

2 Measure across the width of the seat of the chair with the tape measure. Double this measurement and write it down.

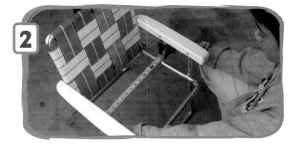

3 Lay out eight-pack rings end to end until their length measures at least the dimension you recorded from step 2. Overlap the rings if you need to.

4 Position and tighten a zip tie at each point where the circles on the eight-pack rings touch. Use the scissors to trim the ends of the zip ties. Repeat steps 3 and 4 to make one or two more rows. The number of rows needed will depend on the size of your chair.

5 Lay the rows next to each other. Position and tighten a zip tie at each point where the circles touch. Use the scissors to trim the ends of the zip ties.

CONTINUED ON NEXT PAGE ➞

6 Lay the plastic mat you have created in step 5 over the chair seat. Wrap it over the chair sides until the ends touch.

7 Use ties to connect the ends of the mat to each other. Also attach the mat to the front of the chair frame. Use a scissors to trim the zip tie ends to complete the chair seat.

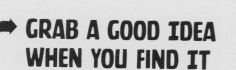

6 IMPROVE

How did your new chair seat work? Try using the same method to make a new back for your chair. Also, try using plastic rings for hammocks or camp stools.

➡ GRAB A GOOD IDEA WHEN YOU FIND IT

Levi Strauss was 24 years old when he headed to California for the gold rush. He brought some canvas cloth with him to sell to the miners. But nobody wanted the cloth. Instead, the miners wanted new pants. So Levi sewed the cloth into pants. The pants sold quickly. They were so durable, everyone wanted a pair. Levi realized he had struck fashion gold with blue jeans!

24

Rain Poncho

1 PROBLEM Every time you go to the store, you bring back plastic shopping bags. No need to send all those bags to a landfill. Can you think of a way to repurpose them?

2 PROPERTIES What useful properties do plastic shopping bags have? They are lightweight. They hold things. They are waterproof. Would any of these properties make the bags useful for something else?

3 IDEAS You could make a kite, a wastebasket liner, a woven plastic mat, or a plastic rain poncho. Bingo! A rain poncho would keep you dry on those rainy days at the park.

4 PLAN

Gather together:
- ✔ scissors
- ✔ 10 heavy duty plastic shopping bags of the same size
- ✔ decorative duct tape
- ✔ measuring tape
- ✔ marker
- ✔ paper

CONTINUED ON NEXT PAGE ➡

5 CREATE

1 Use the scissors to cut the handles from each bag.

2 Lay three of the flattened bags side by side, overlapping sides slightly. Duct tape the sides of the bags together. Turn the bags over, and tape the back sides of the seams as well.

3 Repeat step 2 with three more bags.

4 Use the measuring tape to measure the width of the taped bags along the bottom edge. Write down this measurement.

5 Lay the two rows of bags across from each other. Open edges should face each other. Adjust the bags so that their corners are separated by the distance recorded in step 4.

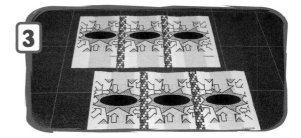

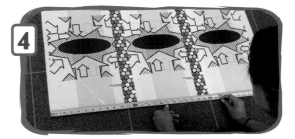

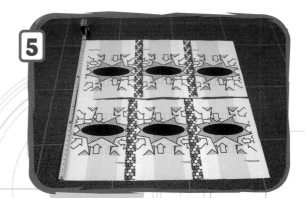

6 Place three of the remaining bags across the gap. Tape the bags together on the front and back seams to make a square.

7 Fold the square from corner to corner to make a triangle.

8 Find the center point along the folded edge by measuring the length of the fold. Then divide this length in half. Make a mark at the center point with the marker.

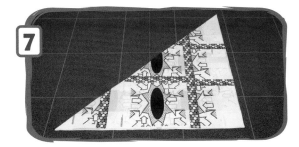

9 Measure and make marks 6 inches (15 cm) on both sides of the center mark.

10 Carefully trim out a narrow strip of plastic between these marks. This action makes a hole for your head.

CONTINUED ON NEXT PAGE ➡

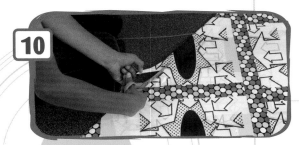

11 Measure and mark 3 inches (8 cm) from each side of this hole along the fold.

12 Measure and mark 30 inches (76 cm) up from the center point of the triangle along both unfolded edges.

13 Draw a line from the mark in step 11 to the mark in step 12 on each side of the head opening. Cut along these lines with a scissors.

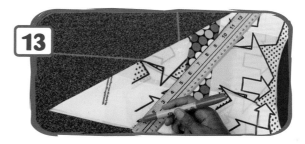

14 Tape along these cuts to make the sides of the poncho.

15 Lay the remaining bag flat. Measure and mark 9 inches (23 cm) from one of the bottom corners along the bottom seam.

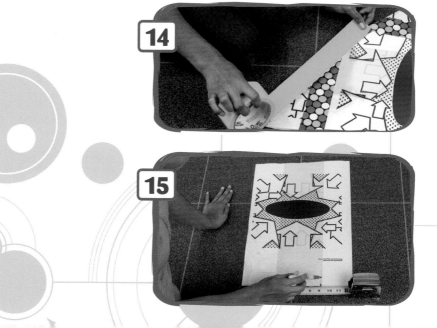

16 Measure and mark 15 inches (38 cm) up from the mark made in step 15.

17 Connect these marks to make a rectangle measuring 9 inches (23 cm) x 15 inches (38 cm). Cut along these lines to make a hood. The bottom of the bag and one side will remain uncut.

18 Overlap the 18-inch (46-cm) cut edge about 1 inch (2.5 cm) with the head opening on the poncho. Center the hood's back seam on the back of the poncho.

19 Smooth and wrap this cut edge around the opening. Tape it in place, inside and out. Seal the front edge of the head opening with tape as well.

20 Your poncho is ready to wear!

Does your poncho fit? What else can you make with plastic shopping bags? Try making a school bag or a tent.

GLOSSARY

biodegradable (by-oh-dee-GRAY-duh-buhl)—a substance or object that breaks down naturally in the environment

compost (KOM-pohst)—mixture of decaying leaves, vegetables, and other items that make the soil better for gardening

condense (kuhn-DENS)—to change from gas to liquid; water vapor condenses into liquid water

cylindrical (si-LIN-drah-cul)—to have flat, circular ends and sides shaped like the outside of a tube

evaporate (i-VA-puh-rayt)—to change from a liquid into a vapor or a gas

fertilize (FUHR-tuh-lyz)—to make soil rich and healthy

natural resource (NACH-ur-uhl REE-sorss)—any substance found in nature that people use, such as soil, air, trees, coal, and oil

repurpose (ri-PUR-puhss)—to find a use for something that is different from what it was intended for

READ MORE

Enz, Tammy. *Build It: Invent New Structures and Contraptions.* Invent It. Mankato, Minn.: Capstone Press, 2012.

Ross, Kathy. *Earth-friendly Crafts: Clever Ways to Reuse Everyday Items.* Minneapolis: Millbrook Press, 2009.

Sirrine, Carol, and Jen Jones. *Teen Crafts: Cool Projects that Look Great and Help Save the Planet.* Green Crafts. Mankato, Minn.: Capstone Press, 2011.

INTERNET SITES

FactHound offers a safe, fun way to find Internet sites related to this book. All of the sites on FactHound have been researched by our staff.

Here's all you do:

Visit *www.facthound.com*

Type in this code: 9781429676366

Check out projects, games and lots more at
www.capstonekids.com

ABOUT THE AUTHOR

Tammy Enz became a civil engineer because of her awe of the massive steel bridges that spanned the Mississippi River. She just had to figure out how they worked. Today, she still likes tinkering and figuring out how things work. When she isn't tinkering, she fixes up old houses and conducts experiments in her garden and kitchen. Most of all, she loves reading books about anything and everything and asking "why?"